THE EDWARD THOMAS COUNTRY

By

W. M. WHITEMAN

Opposite: The Edward Thomas Memorial Stone, Shoulder of Mutton Hill, Steep.

Cover: The drawing of Edward Thomas is based on a sketch by Robin Guthrie.

ISBN 0-86146-067-7

Published by Paul Cave Publications Ltd.,
74 Bedford Place, Southampton.

Printed by Brown & Son (Ringwood) Ltd.,
Crowe Arch lane, Ringwood, Hampshire.

EDWARD THOMAS
(1878-1917)

Philip Edward Thomas, born March 3, 1878, at Lambeth, eldest son of a Board of Trade clerk. Both parents of mainly Welsh blood. Attended various schools, including Board school and St. Paul's. At Oxford 1897-1900, first as non-collegiate student, then at Lincoln College. Married June, 1899 Helen, daughter of James Noble, literary critic. Son, Mervyn, born January, 1900: daughters, Bronwen and Myfanwy, October 1902 and August 1910. Enlisted 1915; commissioned in Royal Garrison Artillery 1916; to France January 1917. Killed at Arras April 9, 1917.

Devoted as a schoolboy to natural history. Encouraged to write by James Noble. Articles published while in 'teens. First book, 'The Woodland Life', at age 19. Leaving Oxford, worked as freelance journalist, book reviewer, writing books on commission and essays. Acquired a reputation as literary critic, especially of contemporary poetry, and as biographer and editor of classics and anthologies. Wrote books on Oxford, Wales, Isle of Wight, the Southern counties, Borrow, Jefferies, Swinburne, Keats, Maeterlinck, the Duke of Marlborough, Celtic and Norse tales, but always in financial stringency. Assiduous country walker. Encouraged by Robert Frost and others, began writing poetry December, 1914. A few poems published 1915-17 under pseudonym 'Edward Eastaway'. First book of poems, as by Edward Thomas, published October, 1917. First complete Collected Poems published in 1949.

Dedication

This book is dedicated to Bill Jarman of Steep who was Edward Thomas's neighbour and bought his bicycle. W.M.W.

(By courtesy of Mrs. Myfanwy Thomas)

EDWARD THOMAS

Preface to the Second Edition

The upsurge of interest in Edward Thomas, his life and works, reached a new height in 1978 with the centenary of his birth. The flood has continued and quickened. More biographical and critical studies have been published, and eminent illustrators engaged. Residual matter by Helen Thomas and Myfanwy has been gathered up. The Oxford University Press produced in 1978 a 368-page edition of the poems, with commentary, the fruit of many years research by Professor George Thomas. Paperback reprints of works long out of print have made the prose more accessible. In bibliographical wealth, in fact, Thomas by far surpasses many greater authors and poets.

A memorial window has been installed in Steep Church, the clear glass engraved by Laurence Whistler with pictorial allusions to the life of Thomas. Admirers have formed an Edward Thomas Fellowship and honour his memory by an annual walk and public readings. 'Admirers', however, is too bloodless a term. His devotees have an enthusiasm and a personal attachment of a kind not commonly found outside Sport and the Theatre, and in literature typical only of a few giants such as Burns or Dickens, and it extends to his family

---

I take this opportunity to revise my interpretation of the poem 'The Other'. Intuitively one indentifies Thomas's double with the Doppelgänger sinister phantom of German folklore. But Thomas's Other is not sinister. Walking ahead of Thomas, he wins acceptance by the country people. Thomas, following, fears their suspicion. I take the poem to be an exploration of Thomas's morbid insecurity and his anxiety over his own personality.

W. M. W.

THE EDWARD THOMAS COUNTRY

WHEN Edward Thomas sat in his study 700 feet up on the hills of East Hampshire, writing against time for his poor living, or relaxing from one of his back-packing long walks, or getting away from domestic ferment, he could look out on a view that calmed his troubled spirit and strengthened the intimations he got from Nature. Below him the hillside plunged into the narrow, dark, mysterious combe, where the tops of beech and yew thrust up to the light, and mists sometimes spiraled up as from a cauldron:

> The Combe was ever dark, ancient and dark.
> Its mouth is stopped with bramble, thorn and briar;
> And no one scrambles over the sliding chalk
> By beech and yew and perishing juniper
> Down the half precipices of its sides.

(The Combe)

In the distance the skyline was a long line of hills, 'sixty miles of South Downs at one glance'. They were hills such as hills ought to be, he felt, such as he would himself make, if he could, to show someone who had never seen any. In the mid-distance he noted the illusion that from the hilltops recreates the dense Wealden forest, although down in the middle of the scene one is aware mainly of fields. Right and left he scanned the wooded hangers that stretch from Langrish to Selborne. Behind him the windswept chalk plateau rose as high as the South Downs. This district north of Petersfield is the Edward Thomas Country, where essentially he found the inspiration and the materials of his poems.

No one locality can claim him exclusively. He was born and brought up in London; publishing and literature kept him linked to it. Both his parents were mainly Welsh, and his affinities with Wales ran deeper than he sometimes admitted. To Wiltshire he had a strong attachment, through visits to relatives and his admiration for Richard Jefferies. But Steep and Froxfield, at the foot and the top of the East Hampshire hangers, had a special place in his life. With his family he had three homes there, from 1906 to 1916, the longest period in his too-short life that he stayed in any district, the period when he produced most of his prose and collected most of the impressions that went into his poetry. Those who know the area and can recognize the references can look on the very sights that inspired him. A large part of the poetry is suffused by the spirit of the place. His memorial, a Sarsen stone or boulder brought from Avebury in Wiltshire, was rightly set up in Steep, high on the hillside which he knew so well, beside a path which he climbed so often.

It was in his mind during his last year, in the Army, when he went on writing poetry, disregarding the lines so that his hut-mates should not see he was writing verse. In 1917, at the age of 39, he could have stayed in home defence, but he volunteered for France. Only a few months before going there, he visited Steep for the last time in, as his friends remembered, a calm readiness to die for England, not from patriotism but from love.

When first I came here I had hope,
Hope for I knew not what. Fast beat
My heart at sight of the tall slope
Of grass and yews, as if my feet
Only by scaling its steps of chalk
Would see something no other hill
Ever disclosed. And now I walk
Down it the last time.

(When First)

If we know Steep, we know that he is walking down the Shoulder of Mutton Hill, one of the steepest climbs in the hangers and recognisable from a great distance by its grassy clearing, shaped more like a mutton chop than a shoulder, with a mass of old yews to the left.

Even in the battle zone his thoughts of Steep were not far away. In the 'Diary of Edward Thomas, 1 January to 8 April, 1917' we read how four or five planes weaving and wheeling overhead reminded him of the kestrels he used to see 'over Mutton and Ludcombe'. Ludcombe or more usually

Lutcombe is the old name for the gorge of the Ashford Stream, the combe of the poem.

The Thomases, with their first two children, came to Hampshire in 1906. They had been turned out of their home near Sevenoaks, in Kent, which was their fourth home since their hurried marriage in 1899. Edward was 28, and making a precarious income from book reviewing and writing commissioned books on subjects not of his choosing. They were attracted to the Petersfield area by what they had heard of the co-educational boarding school Bedales. Helen saw the headmaster, ascertained that the boy Mervyn would be accepted as a day pupil, and then found a cottage in Ashford, about a mile from Bedales by footpath.

Arrival at Berryfield

It was a strikingly beautiful place they came to. Berryfield Cottage lay at the foot of the finest panorama in the whole range of hangers. The very names of the hangers and combes stir something elemental in us. Some of the names are nearly forgotten, but the recital rings out from the past. From Langrish, west of Petersfield, to the Alton road there are Cold Hill, Rothercombe, Great Hanger, Lyth Hanger, Strawberry Hanger, Ridge Hanger, Stoner Hanger, Ashford Hanger and Gudges Hanger. East of the Alton road, within a radius of little more than two miles, are Lutcombe, Ashford Hill, Berryfield Hanger, Shoulder of Mutton Hill, the Warren, Broad Lyth, Wheatham Hill; straggling apart, Coldhayes Hanger, Glascombe Hanger and Flexcombe; then Down Hanger, Juniper Hanger, Ruddlecombe, Oakshott Hanger, Happersnapper Hanger, Roundhills Hanger, Reston Hanger, Doscombe, Farrow Hill and Hawkley Hanger, with the outliers Cheesecombe and Farewell Hanger. Some of these names may be older than Anglo-Saxon.

Thomas delighted in ancient and curious place names rich in associations and suggestions. He proposed Happersnapper Hanger as an alternative when Blackwoods, rejecting his poem 'Lob', flinched at the place name Mother Dunch's Buttocks.

This cliff-like range is part of the broken edge of the chalk that frames the Weald, sweeping from Dover by the North Downs to Farnham and Petersfield and back by the South Downs to Beachy Head. At these edges the land has been heaved up and tilted, so that several strata come to the surface in a short space. The main scarp is chalk, enriched by washings from the clay cap. The mixed soils give the hangers their enchanting mantle of vegetation. In the spring they present a subtly graded spectrum of green, from almost yellow through bright fresh tones to almost black, shot with the grey-brown of beech trunks, the purple-brown of young twigs and flecks of whitebeam silver. The autumn is an explosion of colour — tawny beech, bright gold maple, pale gold oak, ash and willow, sombre dark green yews and hollies, red stems of dogwood, mingled tints of wild privet, sloe, hawthorn and bramble, and the smoky grey of Old Man's Beard.

On the ridge above Berryfield, from the Shoulder of Mutton or Wheatham Hill, the view is even grander than from above the combe, for it is not closed to the south-west by Stoner Hill, and the Downs can be seen to end in their highest point, and Hampshire's, Butser Hill, 888 feet. To the south-east they extend to Cocking and East Lavington, on a very clear day to the Devil's Dyke and Ditchling Beacon.

The scarp twists and writhes through Steep and Oakshott, and its most dramatic feature is the deep indentation of Lutcombe. In 'The South Country' Thomas describes the combes of Hampshire but clearly has this one chiefly in mind. For his book he repudiates any claim to topographical writing. In any case the timetable set by his publisher, Dent, would have excluded the collection of guidebook material, but he also felt that to load his text with names and facts would injure his communication of the spirit of the region. If we are interested in identifications, we must make them for ourselves. The combes, he says, are steep-sided bays, running and narrowing far into and up the sides of the chalk hills, and especially of those hills with which the high flinty plateau breaks down to the greensand and the plain. They are clothed with beech and yew, a few larch, and the white flames of the beam tree buds. Sometimes a stream rises at the head, and before it is a yard wide it is full of trout. The combes are cauldrons for the making and unmaking of mists, and breed families of echoes. They are the home of foxes and owls. The trees bear luxuriant ivy, grey-green lichens and brilliant moss, and their highest branches are hung with cordages of honeysuckle and clematis. This is the very portrait of Lutcombe, except that the trout have left the Ashford Stream.

The Little Switzerland Road

Down the west side of the combe, through what has long been known to tourists as Little Switzerland, runs a well-engineered road made in the 1820s to avoid the gruelling slog up Stoner Hill, straight, steep and stony, but until then, almost unbelievably, the historic coach road to Alton, Winchester and the Midlands. It can be seen branching left, up through the trees, at the foot of the present road. Thomas describes the new road in 'The South

The "mysterious combe" — a view into the depth of Lutcombe from Ashford Hanger.

Country'. 'Every traveller in Hampshire', he writes (but he gives no more positive indication of where), 'remembers the road that sways with airy motion and bird-like curves down from the high land of clay and flint through the chalk to the sand and the river. It doubles round the head of a combe, and the whole descent is through woods uninterrupted and all but impenetrable to the eye above and below except where once or twice it looks through an arrow slit to the blue vale and the castled promontory of Chanctonbury twenty miles south-east. As the road is a mere ledge on the side of a very steep hill the woods below it hurry down to a precipitous pit full of the glimmering, trembling and murmuring of innumerable leaves and no sound or sight of men'.

Thomas tells the story of the new road as local people were telling it sixty years ago. It was made, says the legend, half a century before at the cost of the last of a family which had long owned the manor house. Through his hanging beech woods the road was cut but near the top it needed to go through another property. The owner would not give way, an expensive lawsuit followed, the contract date for the road was passed, the lord of the manor was ruined and had to sell his whole estate. Thomas gives a graphic description of all he had to leave behind, including his white house by the rivulet and its chain of pools, his high fruit walls, and his Spanish chestnuts above the rocky lane. It could not be plainer that we are in Ashford. When the Ashford gardens are opened nowadays for charity, the chain of pools through which the Ashford Stream runs behind the high walls arouses the delight of visitors. The Spanish chestnuts are still there, growing with limes and beeches on top of the banks of the sunken approach lane. Thick, gnarled, with some branches amputated, they are probably remnants of a 400-year-old avenue to the Tudor manor house, similar to that at Halnaker House near Goodwood. The white house is gone, burned down it is said, but the modern house keeps alive the name Old Ashford Manor.

As usual with local legends, the tale is mixed truth and error. The road is earlier than Thomas was told. The turnpike Act providing for this improvement was passed in 1825. The old family at Ashford, the Bakers, who had been there from Tudor times, had sold it by 1810, and the chief promoter of the new road was the buyer, a Londoner named Moses Hoper, from the fashionable Mayfair quarter, who married a Petersfield girl and with her father's help bought the estate with its farms. Hoper was a rash or unlucky speculator. Farm rents slumped after the Napoleonic War, and Ashford was heavily mortgaged. Road

Opposite: Ashford Stream, Steep.

making was his final ruin. He was fearful that the champions of the direct Petersfield to Winchester road, who also got their Act in 1825, would carry out their improvements first, and he probably assumed too much of the burden of the Ashford route himself. It seems there was a lawsuit, and in 1827 he was a broken man. The whole estate was sold to a big landowner in Yorkshire who never, as far as we know, came to look at it.

Records of the law suit are lacking, It is true that at Week Green the new road had to pass through William Harmsworth's land, but Harmsworth was among the trustees named in the Act. It may be that what he was resisting was a private road being cut at the same time by Hoper to link Ashford with a farm of his at the top. This road can be seen veering off the public road near the bend called Cold Corner, but near the top there is no sign of completion. The keen eye of Thomas did not miss this track, but he thought it might be an older road part of which was incorporated in the zigzag.

On the downhill side of the gently graded road, as it descends through Ashford Hanger, is a bank, that in the poem 'The Path':

> Running along a bank, a parapet
> That saves from the precipitous wood below
> The level road, there is a path. It serves
> Children for looking down the long smooth steep,
> Between the legs of beech and yew

The parallels with Thomas's earlier description of the combe and the road are marked, and the whole poem is a vivid description of the road. Eleanor Farjeon describes how, when the Thomas children went up from Steep to meet their father coming from his study on the ridge, the youngest, Myfanwy, loved to run along this bank. Though anyone can now look safely at the long views from prepared parking places, unwary motor cars sometimes overshoot the bends and plunge down the slope.

Steep

Below the scarp, Steep is an area of scattered farms and a few large houses, Victorian or later, standing in their own grounds and built when the gentry took over from the yeoman class. The hedged fields, arable or pasture, are irregular or regular according as they date from the first clearing and colonising or from later enclosures, perhaps for Tudor or Stuart sheep flocks, perhaps for the agrarian revolution of the eighteenth and nineteenth centuries. Many patches of wood and copse survive, saved at one time for timber and small wood, for charcoal, and for windbreaks, though today no hazel copse is worked in Steep, even for firewood. Hurdles and basketwork are lost local crafts. Thomas knew those copses, tempting, he observed, to mouse and wren, blackbird and robin:

> There they stand, on their ends, the fifty faggots
> That once were underwood of hazel and ash
> In Jenny Pink's Copse.
>
> (Fifty Faggots)

Pinks Copse is a Steep place name, at the top of Ridge Hanger.

Just as characteristic of Steep as the tremendous slopes are the little yellow Celandines that grow profusely in the wet lands which are maintained, in spite of Victorian land drainage, by countless springs and streams from the chalk massif. Delicately formed, they spread bravely and sparkle with gold flowers. No other modest ground cover proclaims more confidently the arrival of spring. The motif of the poem 'Celandine' is one of Thomas's dream maidens, but the familiar happy plants provide the counterpoint. The flower has normally eight petals, sometimes more or fewer. Only Thomas, one fancies, would have noticed, among thousands, one with only five petals, and have mentioned it without losing the poetry in mere botany. And has any other poet perceived the beauty of the lacey fronds of the wayside Cow Parsley (It Rains)?

Thomas's delight in place names, through which he felt linked with unnumbered earlier generations, is expressed touchingly, and with a gaiety very rare to his writings, in the group of poems in which his mind plays over the appeal of the English countryside and the romance of its names, and he contemplates the gifts he would make to his children. In one of them is the only direct reference to Steep. The music and the metre have a ballad lilt well suited to the simple emotions:

> If I should ever by chance grow rich
> I'll buy Codham, Cockridden, and Childerditch,
> Roses, Pyrgo, and Lapwater,
> And let them all to my elder daughter.

Most of the places he names in the three poems are from Essex, near Colchester, Chelmsford and Brentwood, where his Army training took him, but for the younger daughter Myfanwy, after running over the possibilities, he decides:

> Her small hands I would not cumber
> With so many acres and their lumber
> But leave her Steep and her own world
> And her spectacled self with her hair uncurled.

The group ends with a poem 'And You, Helen', in a different mood. It treats of his recurring agonising thought that he had failed his wife. She is a very loving and always ready support, and he has not given her what she needs but somehow damaged her. He aches to do things for her but is inhibited. But that is not the road we are following here.

The Road of Life

A feature of Steep is the close network of roads, narrow lanes and paths, many showing their age by the extent to which they are worn down. Especially on uphill hauls, where the wheels of heavily laden waggons and the carts have ground through the surface, and rainwater has deepened the channels, the lanes are so sunken that the banks may reach ten or fifteen feet up to the adjoining fields. Thomas was not greatly interested in their history or archaeology. That is apparent from his book on the Icknield Way. Roads meant something else to him.

In the prose he sees them sometimes with the eyes of an inveterate walker. He girds like any modern rambler, in a piece on roads in 'The South Country', at the loss of old roads, deserted and surviving only as tunnels under the hazels, 'like Sandsbury Lane near Petersfield — because straight new roads have taken their place for the purposes of tradesmen and carriage people'. Sandsbury Lane ran from the tithing of Aldersnapp to the hamlet of Dunhill, both in Steep, but was closed in 1866. Thomas must have heard the local story that the landowner was allowed to close it in exchange for land to make the present road from Steep to Stroud, but he was misled. That road is far older than the closure of the lane. Tradition, however, rarely tells complete lies. Landed interest may have been at work, for the owner at both ends of the lane was the local MP, John Bonham-Carter II. The carriage people kept it for themselves. There died recently an old lady who remembered driving to Steep church along Sandsbury Lane from the big house where she then lived.

In the poems, roads have a deeper significance, and in Steep Thomas must constantly have been reminded of it. They attracted him as symbols of human destiny. The image of the road expressed his brooding sense of time and fate, his foreboding of the future. For him the cross-roads is not a stale metaphor. At a four-went way — the term is his — three roads go off we know not where. What happens, if, in Time's irrevocability, we take one road rather than another? Thomas would have appreciated the simile of J. W. Dunne, in 'An Experiment with Time', where he likens time in the first level of consciousness to a road along which a man walks. The man is in the present, behind him is the known past, ahead is the to-him unknown future. But the whole length of the road exists timelessly.

Forest — a universal symbol of deep psychological significance — and road are the main motifs in one of Thomas's finest but most pessimistic poems, 'Lights Out':

> I have come to the borders of sleep,
> The unfathomable deep
> Forest where all must lose
> Their way, however straight
> Or winding, soon or late;
> They cannot choose.
> Many a road and track
> That since the dawn's first crack
> Up to the forest brink
> Deceived the travellers,
> Suddenly now blurs,
> And in they sink.

At a time when Thomas had produced only prose, W. H. Hudson wrote to Edward Garnett, another friend, the much quoted words 'I believe he has taken the wrong path and is wandering lost in the vast wilderness. He is essentially a poet'. That was penetrating. It expressed Thomas's situation in Thomas's own images.

In the poem 'The Other', which evokes in the reader an uncomfortable sympathy with Thomas, the road theme is joined to his fear of inner conflict. The poet emerges from the forest and follows the road happily until he comes to an inn where he hears of someone, the double of himself, who has preceded him. Fearful, he hastens after the stranger, and gets news of him at inn after inn, always a little way ahead. At last he catches up, in time to hear, in a tap-room, the Other loudly complaining that Thomas, dreaming of him, running after him, is hounding and persecuting him. Thomas hastily withdraws, but is unable to give up:

> He goes: I follow: no release
>
> Until he ceases. Then I also shall cease.

The Doppelgänger of German folklore springs to mind. But the Dopplegänger is a sinister phantom that presages death; Thomas's double is human and liked by the country people. Pursuer and pursued are two aspects of the same. Thomas was obsessed by fear that because of some personal inadequacy no one liked him. Inns were for him symbols of the friendly communities from which he felt excluded.

Black Shadows

All writers on Thomas refer to his melancholy. He used the word himself. But melancholy is a calm, contemplative, self-indulgent mood. It can be savoured, as it was by Robert Burton and Shakespeare's Jaques. Thomas's was a deeply disturbing unease. He suffered all his life, with intermittent and brief periods of relief, from a haunting insecurity and distrust of his ability to reach the high standards he set himself. It is not too strong to say that over long periods he was hag-ridden. Some have attributed his black moodiness to his Celtic descent, which seems unjust to the Welsh. In fact, in his circumstances there was an appalling combination of classic causes of insecurity more than enough to account for his mental and emotional stresses, and even for his headaches and spells of exhaustion.

A stern Nonconformist father with whom he could not communicate, who had fought his way up from poverty to a higher cultural and rather unsure social standing, and was over-anxious that his son should not slip back; a mother loving and caring but inarticulate; four childhood homes and five different schools; the ex-Board school boy at the prestigious grammar school, isolated there by his sense of social inferiority, his poorer clothes, and his unorthodox interests; continuation of this isolation during his first year at Oxford, with only non-collegiate status — against all those odds, with a mind of high quality and proud sensitivity, he struggled out of his despised, cramped, lower middle class background into an intellectual, literary and artistic world which was congenial but cut him off from his roots and made him distrustful of his powers. That was bound to produce disorientation. And then he had to shoulder, too early and too much, the responsibilities of husband, father and breadwinner, unsupported by his father, when barely

Opposite: Wheatham Hill, seen from Stoner Hill.

out of his undergraduate phase, and with a wife to whom he was devoted but felt under obligations.

It was not melancholy but anguish, not a mood but a torturing and recurring sickness of mind, that drove him to think of suicide and breaking up his marriage. No man could have borne it for a full lifetime. Had he not been killed on the Western Front he must either have come through his private hell or have killed himself.

One can see the marks of stress in the photographs of him, especially those taken after some ten years of struggle to support a family. The features are delicate and suggest a sensitive, intellectual and aesthetic make-up, but the face is lean, hawk-like and strong. The expression, however, contains more than a hint of sadness and pain.

In his unease he found balm, as well as food for self-communion, in the countryside, and especially in the older settled regions of England. The south of England, Hampshire not least, is a benign country, where Man and Nature have lived together a very long time. Over the millenia they have learned to co-operate and not fear each other. Man shaped the hills and fields, and they in turn moulded him. When Thomas brooded in his hill-top hide above the combe, or gazed at the Downs from Wheatham Hill, or let his senses dwell on lichens or pewits, the smell of woodbine or the ripples of silver in the green of the windblown grass, it helped to calm him. It did more. It nourished his almost religious sense of belonging to the very soil of England and being part of its continuity.

His acute observation of Nature began in a schoolboy interest in natural history, practised on the fringe of South London. His 'country' prose written when a young man is often forced and stilted, too consciously aiming at the purple passage or the affected phrase. But the discipline of producing uncongenial commissioned work, mostly to firm deadlines, dragged him past that. By the time he settled in Steep he had developed a vision that penetrated below surfaces, and a sureness of touch in his management of words. His prose book most relevant here, 'The South Country', lacks construction and is padded out with inexcusable digressions, but there is no doubting the intense sincerity of his descriptions of Nature and landscape or the extent to which they moved him. What his eyes, ears and nose brought him, he apprehended with the tentacles of the spirit. Though his kind of perennial disquiet is of northern Europe, there is a Buddhistic quality in his recognition of the unity of life and the

Opposite: Steep and the South Downs, from the hangers above Berryfield.

value of all its elements, great and small. In 'The South Country', after describing the song of the nightingale, he refers to the mysterious sense that 'there are things not human yet of great power and honour in the world'. That word 'honour' is illuminating. Only a finely tuned spirit would sense that respect and humility, and not only admiration, are due to the nightingale's song.

It is absurd that Edward Thomas should ever have been classed as a Pastoral, a Georgian or a Soldier Poet. He is unique. But if he must be classified, he stands, though less serene and nearer to earth, with the mystics Blake and Traherne. He would have said with Traherne

To walk abroad is, not with eyes,

But thoughts, the fields to see and prize.

and, again in 'The South Country', he has two long quotations from Traherne, including the words 'Eternity was manifest in the light of the day, and something infinite behind everything appeared, which tallied with my expectation and moved my desire'.

Of Ashford, set in the midst of Nature and in the heart of southern England, Thomas wrote to his friend the poet Gordon Bottomley that it was 'the most beautiful place we have ever lived in. We are now become people of whom passers-by stop to think: How fortunate are they within those walls. I know it. I have thought the same as I came to the house and forgot it was my own'.

Ten years later Thomas used that thought in his poem 'Wind and Mist', but transferred the connection to his next house, half a mile away on the Froxfield ridge, for he mentions the view — 'angled fields of grass and grain bounded by oak and thorn' and 'sixty miles of South downs at one glance'. That view is not to be seen from Berryfield. In his poems Thomas often has strangers met in chance encounters. In this poem a stranger asks

'That house, though modern, could not be better planned
For its position. I never liked a new
House better. Could you tell me who lives in it?'.
'No one'. 'Ah — and I was peopling all
Those windows on the south with happy eyes,
The terrace under them with happy feet;
Girls —'. 'Sir, I know. I know. I have seen that house
Through mist look lovely as a castle in Spain
And airier. I have thought: 'twere happy there
To live. And I have laughed at that
Because I lived there then'.

Edward Thomas's first home in Hampshire — Berryfield Cottage, Ashford, Steep.

Berryfield Cottage

Berryfield Cottage was all they could have hoped for, friendly, domestic, restful. It is a farmhouse in the local vernacular style — malmstone with bricks at the corners and framing the doors and windows, and tiled roof. 'Malmstone' is the name given to the stone, in character something between sandstone and chalk, which was formerly quarried in the Upper Greensand at the foot of the hangers. It is soft when cut, hence the need for brick reinforcement, but hardens with exposure.

The house dates from 1820, when Moses Hoper created the farm of 63 acres out of the Ashford estate and built the house, with barn, cowshed, stable, carthouse, piggery and the rest. At first the farm was called formally Ashford Farm, and informally New Farm. Later it was styled New House Farm. The name Berryfield Cottage is derived from two of the farm's fields on the other side of the lane, Great Berryfield and Little Berryfield, and was no doubt introduced some time after the farm was consolidated in a larger holding, and the farmhouse, no longer required for its original purpose, became a separate residence.

Ashford was a 'reputed manor' of uncertain origin, separated to some extent from the Bishop of Winchester's great manor of East Meon in the fourteenth century. For a long time it had a manor house near the ford of the Ashford Stream, one of the most vigorous of the Rother's tributaries. As was usual, it was farmhouse as well as chief residence, but Hoper, buying for investment and not wishing to live there, let it, with its outbuildings, curtilage, paddocks and orchards, as a gentleman's home, and built the new farmhouse farther east.

The farmhouse, now cottage, faces west, its garden sideways-on to the lane. Northward is the great backcloth of the hangers; Berryfield Hanger and the Shoulder of Mutton, to the right Wheatham Hill, to the left the deep re-entrant of Lutcombe descending from the rim of the scarp at Week Green to the site of the ford. New House Farm occupied a shelf from which the ground dropped sharply to a lower reach of the stream, which ran through water meadows and watercress beds before turning south to the ponds of the old Ashford Mill, also called Steep Mill. The barn can still be seen, converted into a gatehouse to Ashford Chace.

From Berryfield, Mervyn could walk through the woods and fields to Bedales, past the waterfall of the mill, by this time only pumping water to one of the big houses, and emerge opposite Steep Church along an old road, now only a footpath, across the common.

Helen's Story

For the Thomases' ten years in the area, Helen's own narrative is tantalising. It is in two parts, 'As It Was' (1926), said to have been written as a therapeutic exercise after a breakdown, and 'World Without End' (1931), dealing respectively with her life with Edward up to and after the birth of Mervyn. Its content is autobiographical, and generally it has been accepted without much question, but its purpose is to tell a love story, not to relate facts. It has, for example, no dates. The form is fictional. The characters are given other names — Edward and Helen become David and Jenny, Edward's father is Mr. Townsend, Eleanor Farjeon is Margaret — or they are not named at all. Even Robert Frost, one of Edward's closest friends, whose influence on his turning to poetry was crucial, is merely 'an American'. Places are not named, and the reader knows simply that he is in Hampshire not far from Selborne. Only if he has first hand acquaintance with the area can he, from the internal evidence, locate where the Thomases lived.

This raises the question of how much is reliable. The disguise may be thin, but by presenting her story in this way. Helen has served notice on us that she must not be attacked if we find some parts have been re-shaped creatively, or touched up by the writer's craft. The boundary between biography and imaginative work is blurred. However, while we may regret the omissions, questions of accuracy are not very important. They arise mainly in relationships between people. In her descriptions of the Steep scene she is an acute observer and shows a flair for graphic reporting. Given the same aim, Edward could not have done much better.

While he, reserved and preoccupied, remained aloof, Helen eagerly joined the Bedales circle. The school was more than an educational establishment. It was the chief generator of forces in Steep, and an important if divisive community focus. There was no squire in the neighbourhood. The successor to Ashford, the largest estate, was a minor. The gentry influence was divided between a small group of 'ladies of the parish'. As a conspicuous embodiment of advancing ideas, Bedales was bound to be an exciting, disturbing and indigestible element in a loosely knit rural society.

John Haden Badley, the founder and headmaster, started the school in Sussex in 1893 and moved it to Steep in 1900, taking over and expanding the big Victorian house Steephurst, which had replaced the old Church Farm. With it went 150 acres, mostly farmed. Badley had something of a Moses in his make-up, authoritarian and self-confident in his ideals. But in its reaction against High Victorian stuffiness, the progressive movement had shown an inevitable extremism. In greater or less degree Bedales had all the ingredients — co-education, the simple life, disciplinary rigours, the open air, hygiene, Ruskin and Morris, arts and crafts, Liberty dresses, folk dancing, vegetarianism, teetotalism, pacifism, intellectual liberalism, pink middle class socialism, votes for women, moral earnestness. It was well-rounded, but to a narrow model. To the established order it was at once ridiculous and alarming.

Helen, in many ways unconventional, was at first very much at home in this company. She mixed with the staff, parents and sympathizers, worked part-time teaching infants, took in children unable to join their parents for holidays, attended discussion meetings, and addressed some. Later she had a revulsion of feeling against the 'Bedales people'. There is more than objective disapproval in her bitter criticism. Something had touched her on the raw.

Delighted as Edward was with Berryfield in 1906, it was a blow when in 1908 it became apparent that the Ashford estate would be broken up and sold. He had no money to buy the cottage and might have to leave. However in September he wrote Gordon Bottomley that a friend had promised to build them a house at the top of the hangers. He was used to frequent moves. In their eighteen years of married life, he and Helen had nine different homes, without counting temporary accommodation. He regarded a move almost as a magical way to a new start, and for a short period it gave him confidence and new cheer.

Lupton the Builder

The friend was an Old Bedalian, an ardent young Yorkshireman named Geoffrey Lupton, aged about 26, who had absorbed the teachings of William Morris and formed an affection for the Bedales countryside. Abandoning a career in the wealthy family engineering business, he trained under Ernest Gimson, a leading figure in the arts and crafts movement, and then returned to Steep to live and work there as a furniture maker, joiner and builder. In 1908 he was completing his house and workshops near Week Green, overlooking the deep re-entrant of Lutcombe. They were later occupied by Edward Barnsley, the distinguished furniture designer and maker, who was Lupton's apprentice.

Lupton's most important building work was the hall and library of Bedales, both designed by Ernest Gimson, with superb interior woodwork like a mediaeval barn. The Lupton Hall he built at his own cost in 1911, the Memorial Library (1920-21) after Gimson's death. In 1908 he was still getting established. Eager to practise and develop his skills, and taking a liking to Thomas, he offered to build him a house a little farther along the ridge. The proposal included a small building between the two houses and slightly down the slope, part of which Edward could use as a study. The study was finished first, in March 1909, and Edward moved his books in. It had a thatched roof and two non-connecting rooms separated by a fireplace, the second room being for Lupton. Later known as the Bee House because Lupton stored his bee-keeping equipment there, it has twice been enlarged as a complete house, and the original form is not recognisable. The Thomases' house was finished in December, when they moved in.

Its designer was Alfred Powell, a colleague of Gimson's and brother of the second master at Bedales, for whom he designed a house near the school, Little Hawsted. The two houses, with Mansard roof and long, low look, have a family resemblance. Into the execution of the Thomas house Lupton put his philosophy, his best materials, and his craftsmanship. The structure is of local hand-made bricks and tiles, with massive oak framing timbers inside. The doors of solid oak, having fittings of wrought iron made in Lupton's own smithy. Floors are oak planks or twelve-inch Sussex tiles. In the sitting room at the east end, with windows on three sides, the planks are two inches thick and up to thirty-two

Opposite: The Ashford hangers. In centre, the distinctive clearing on the Shoulder of Mutton Hill.

inches wide. Lupton was satisfying his own criteria virtually regardless of cost. At the back (south) the two storeys stand the height of three because of the slope, and at the foot of this south wall is a long paved terrace, with the built-in alcove and seat for which Helen asked.

John Moore, in his book on Thomas's life and letters, says the builder friend came to the rescue when the Thomases had to quit Berryfield. 'About this time', he writes, 'the estate on which Berryfield Cottage stood was sold to a rich man who planned to build a great house on the dandelion field, using Berryfield itself as a gardener's lodge'. This is based on Helen. She seems to have re-arranged events for literary reasons. The move to Froxfield was planned and the Thomases' new house started before the Ashford heiress came of age and proceeded to sell off her inheritance. The rich man did not come on the scene until late 1910, and his big new house was built in 1912. Can it have been contemplated in 1908?

Lord of the Manor

The new master of Ashford was Aubyn Bernard Rochfort Trevor-Battye, naturalist, artist, traveller and explorer. He is known to Hampshire people as responsible for the natural history section of their Victoria County History, but he was also natural history editor-in-chief for the whole series. He pulled down most of the house, Ashford Lodge as it was called after a late Georgian rebuilding. It was dilapidated and he decided to build elsewhere. In Tudor times or earlier the site near the ford had been chosen for its ample water supply, but by 1911 the criteria were different. The site was a cold pocket, and it did not command the views enjoyed from other parts of the estate. The natural platform occupied by New House Farm was an ideal ready-made site, with a south prospect over falling ground and the stream, and a north prospect towards the hangers. Here he built his new and larger house, Ashford Chace.

Though often absent on his travels, Trevor-Battye liked the role of lord of the manor. The aggrandisement of the manor of Ashford that appears in the gazetteer information in Kelly's Directory coincidentally with its occupation by Trevor-Battye must have been based on information supplied by him, and he was more proprietorial than his predecessors. There was friction later, about 1913, when young guests of the Thomases, as Eleanor Farjeon relates, took down and burned one of his notices to trespassers in what she calls the Stoner Gorge. 'May the fumes suffocate Squire Trevor-Battye, arch-enemy of ancient rights of way', she wrote. From her description, however, it appears that

The Red House, Froxfield, Edward Thomas's second home in Hampshire.

the sign was not barring any right of way but was aimed at people descending into the private woods from the zigzag public highway. Edward had a different resentment. Towards the end of 'The South Country' he makes a second protest at the closure of Sandsbury Lane, though this time it is an unnamed lane 'a little north of Petersfield'. And then he denounces the barbed wire 'fastened into the living trees alongside the footpath over a neighbouring hill that has lately been sold'. This sounds like the footpath that climbs Ashford Hill from the Stream. His complaint is that strict preservation of the adjoining private woodland spoils his enjoyment of the public footpath. What', he asks, 'is the value of every one's right to use a footpath if a single anti-social landowning citizen has the right to make it intolerable except to such as consider it a place only for the soles of the feet.'

Misunderstanding has become attached to the name Week Green, which Thomas spelt Wick Green. It is not the name of his house. That seems to have had no name until the 1920s, when it was called the Red House. When Thomas put 'Wick Green' at the head of his notepaper he was merely stating where he was writing from, as in earlier and later years he wrote from 'The Weald' or from 'Steep'. Week Green is, or rather was, a small common at the head of the Ashford Gorge, the Lutcombe re-entrant, with two ponds and an old farmhouse. Seven ways, old and modern, met there, including two lateral routes that look like ancient tracks. Cockshott Lane, on which Lupton's house and the Red House both stand, is one of them.

Someone told Edward Week Green was a mis-spelling by the Ordnance Survey, and that Wick Green was correct. Week, like the variant Wyke, is a later form of the Early English *wick*, which usually means a cattle farm, but it was a well-established form at least as far back as the 1750s, and it has the merit of helping to distinguish Week Green Farm, at the road junction, from Wyke Green Farm, three hundred yards to the south-west.

At the foot of the combe is a tree that may be the very one that Thomas saw in 'Man and Dog'. His old man stares up at the mistletoe that hangs too high in the poplar's crest to be plundered. In our day it is possible, before Christmas, to find a man climbing it. Not quite as daringly as the old man did when he fell and broke his leg; the modern raider has climbing irons and tackle.

The Chalk Streams

Farther east there is no easy descent of the scarp, as William Cobbett found, trying to get to Hindhead and obstinately refusing all directions via Liphook. The edge of the plateau drops suddenly to Froxfield's lowland sector, the tithing of Oakshott, embraced between the promontories of Farrow Hill and Wheatham Hill. In this area, in 'May the twenty-third', the poet meets old Jack Noman, who is a re-appearance of the Watercress Man from the prose work 'Heart of England'. He wears cowslips from Wheatham Hill in his cap and buttonhole, and carries watercress from Oakshott Stream in his basket. Today the watercress industry in these parts is concentrated in huge commercial beds at Alresford, but in Thomas's day good crops were gathered at Steep and Oakshott. The chalk rivers of Hampshire, with their pure, clean water, emerging filtered and at a constant temperature of 51 degrees Fahrenheit from the chalk, create ideal conditions. Marketing has changed, however, and now there are only patches of the cress gone to weed in the Ashford and Oakshott Streams. Cowslips too have become rarer on the hangers. They have been trampled, over-picked and dug up. The primroses survive better.

The chalk of Froxfield and Steep was extensively used in the past to lighten the clay soils, and there are at least five large chalk pits. The largest, a considerable quarry known as My Lady's Garden, is hidden in the woods on Ashford Hill. The one in 'The Chalk Pit', however, is most likely that at the foot of Wheatham Hill. Along its rim an ancient road climbs, probably pre-Roman, making for Old Litten Lane and Week Green:

Is this the road that climbs above and bends
Round what was once a chalk-pit: now it is
By accident an amphitheatre . . .
. . . It is called the Dell.
They have not dug chalk here for a century.

This is the pit most like an amphitheatre. Until after the Great War it was a favourite camping ground for Gypsies, and was called Dell, 'dell' meaning originally not a leafy hollow but a hole or pit.

Though it is not explicit, there is a recurring note of sadness in the poems on the countryside. Old friendly things are passing. The chalk pit is finished. The Mill (The Mill-Water) has gone, and there is only the mill-fall 'where once men had a work-place and a home'. The barn, in the poem of that name, is abandoned. The woodland is neglected. In the hangers, where the steep slopes make timber extraction costly,

Lichen, ivy and moss
Keep evergreen the trees
That stand half-flayed and dying,
And the dead trees on their knees
In dog's mercury and moss.

(The Hollow Wood)

Since Thomas's day the dog's mercury and wild garlic have greatly spread, crowding out the bluebells.

Nettles appear where man has disturbed the ground and then given up the fight, and in Steep and Froxfield, where many small farms have been merged in larger, and their buildings left unwanted,

Tall nettles cover up, as they have done
These many springs, the rusty harrow, the plough
Long worn out, and the roller made of stone:
Only the elm butt tops the nettles now

(Tall Nettles)

The poem 'Haymaking', a piece of picture making, ends with a kind of awareness that the writer is watching the end of an epoch for agricultural England.

Thomas at Ease

The transience of things found an echo in his temperament. Those who knew Thomas have recorded that he was shy, reserved and serious, and rarely smiled. The descriptions we have of him relaxed and happy, mainly with his children, are regrettably few. With a few old friends, especially those from the literary world, he could be contentedly intimate. With a few kindred spirits he was sometimes merry. One of them lived at Oakshott. This was Harry Roberts, a vivid personality of enormous energy who combined a large medical practice in Stepney, where he was regarded as a kind of saint, with an open air life in Oakshott and Petersfield, recreational if anything but leisured, spent in a great variety of physical and cultural pursuits and unaffected good works. He was later a close friend of Lord Horder's when the latter moved to Ashford Chace.

In the biography 'Doctor Himself', by Winifred Stamp, there is a happy sketch of Edward Thomas, 'a slight, shy fair man, with a low and pleasant voice,' who was introduced to Roberts by Lupton. 'We liked him at once; he fitted in with our new house and our new country surroundings as easily as did birds and bushes . . . He became a frequent visitor and would sit in the firelight in our rather bare big room talking to Harry or singing Welsh songs in a clear, pure, slight voice which matched his physique to perfection. He and Harry were a pair of opposites: Harry dark, never still, vital and dynamic in every movement and thought; Thomas quiet, often depressed, contemplative and delicately observant, as unobtrusive as Harry was emphatic. Yet they liked one another, though they argued a lot.'

A much closer friend, with a common interest in literature, was James Guthrie, founder of the private Pear Tree Press, who lived eight miles away at Harting. Thomas often walked over to see him. When Guthrie moved to Flansham, near Bognor, Thomas would walk the twenty miles to Chichester and meet Guthrie at the Cross. From there they walked another ten miles to Flansham, and Thomas might, on impulse, stop the night. Guthrie's description of Thomas's personality, of his mannerisms such as sitting sideways at table with his legs crossed, of the felicity and distinction of his conversation, is a vivid and moving tribute of friendship and affection. It appears in his privately printed and rare work 'To the Memory of Edward Thomas', 1937.

Thomas, says Guthrie, had a great gift of making and keeping friends. The judgement is supported by the remarkable gallery of poets, men of letters, journalists and artists who knew and warmed to him. They included Walter de la Mare, H. W. Nevinson, Robert Frost, W. H. Hudson, W. H. Davies, Gordon Bottomley, John Freeman, Joseph Conrad, Hilaire Belloc, Lascelles Abercrombie, Norman Douglas, D. H. Lawrence, Rupert Brooke, Arthur Ransome and Muirhead Bone. yet this was a man who felt himself so isolated from the social groups around him that, as he wrote to Bottomley, social intercourse was to him only an intense form of solitude, and so insecure that, imagining his epitaph, he declared that he had loved no one.

With this reserve and unease, it must have been an intriguing personality that impressed and won all those men, and led so many to publish their memories of him. The word 'beauty' was used of his face and accepted as strictly factual, and according to Ashley Gibson, a hardened Fleet Street journalist, in the streets of London strangers turned round to gaze after him, not for his country cousin clothing but for his bodily distinction and his other-worldly bearing. This personality comes through to us, and has made Thomas a legend when many greater poets remain shadowy.

Outside his intellectual equals Thomas did not easily make contact. For all his absorption in the countryside, he was not a countryman but a countrygoer, a wayfarer. He did not identify with the rural society and economy, or even take much note of it. The country people of his poems are mostly met singly and, like Wordsworth's, are creatures of art and imagination more than flesh and blood. They are character parts, like Jack Noman, or Farmer Hayward in 'Women He Liked'; or they are figures in the landscape, there not in their own right but to complete the composition or as catalysts to start the poet's reflections. Sometimes they air thoughts and feelings that he is shy of expressing as his own. But he was a good reporter too, and did not miss realities. The Gypsy with her baby and her mouth-organ-playing brother may be romantic figures from Borrow's world, but we do not doubt that he saw a Gypsy with pink sham flowers, and in his day many southern Gypsies, even the prosperous ones he saw at Goodwood races, were, as he indicates, living in hooped tents not caravans.

The Heath

A lively passage under 'Hampshire', at the end of 'The South Country', is perhaps Thomas's only full sketch of a rural society at work or play. It describes a fair. As usual the setting is not named, but we are unmistakably reading an account of the October Taro Fair on Petersfield Heath. His common is small, whereas Petersfield Heath is large, but the sandy soil, the large pond, the tumuli, the golf house, the Downs three miles away — all that is the Heath. The crowds, the children, the beggars and Gypsies, the showmen's caravans, roundabouts, side shows and flags, the cakes and ale, bulls and bullocks, auction sales of horses, and Irish dealers haggling apart to avoid the auctioneers' charges are well-remembered elements in Taro Fair recorded in many photographs and water-colours treasured by Petersfield people.

Thomas in his writings identifies several places to the south of his Hampshire homes. In 'The South Country' he names Buriton, the home of Gibbon, as well as the statue of William III at Petersfield, and in 'Four-and-Twenty Blackbirds', his charming tales for children written, so Helen says, before they moved to Steep, we find Petersfield Heath, Chalton, the Coach and Horses, an inn on the Portsmouth road near Butser, Goose Green on the Sussex border, and Sheet, where the boys in one tale find a hundred sand martins' nests. But Steep and Froxfield, from which he drew so much, are hardly ever mentioned. When he responded most creatively to his environment, he preferred anonymity.

The White Horse

In the poems an unusually long burst of human interest is found in 'Up in the Wind', the first poem Thomas wrote apart from schoolboy experiments. It has for its unnamed setting the White Horse public house, on the Froxfield plateau though in the parish of Prior's Dean. Sheltered by a clump of trees, a feature conspicuous in the landscape of the plateau, it is strangely Isolated in the middle of fields, aside from the roads. The explanation is that before the common of Froxfield, called the Barnet, was enclosed and farmed, an old road from Alton to Petersfield, through East Tisted and Colemore, came across the plateau past the inn, where a smithy and a pond met some other needs of eighteenth century travellers.

William Cooke, in his Critical Biography, has reported an unpublished prose treatment of the subject entitled 'The White House', written in November 1914. Thomas's friend, the American poet Robert Frost, had advised him to re-make some of his prose as poetry, and here is Thomas doing that. A fortnight or so after the prose essay he wrote the poem. We can look over his shoulder as he takes Frost's advice.

He paints the scene, the isolation, the wilderness, the wind in the trees, two calves wading in the pond, the call of the curlew, and, inside, the 'wild girl', returned from the slums of London, scrubbing the floor while cabbage bubbles in the big saucepan on the fire. She tells him how her great-uncle, a sawyer from the Shires, came to Froxfield to cut wood for the charcoal burners, and married the widow of the blacksmith, who had set up the alehouse when her husband died. The girl's father, who came as a boy with his uncle, stayed on. That is the story in the poem, but there is reason to think the inn is much older, and was trading simultaneously with the smithy, now the lounge bar. Two or three hundred years ago this now-lost road was an important one from Sussex to Newbury, Oxford and the Midlands. There would have been a demand for refreshment for man and beast, not only repairs.

The White Horse, Prior's Dean. The scene of Edward Thomas's poem 'Up in the Wind'. The old smithy is on the right of the picture.

The inn of the poem has no signboard, only the post and frame. The sign, says the girl, was stolen and thrown in the pond, and remained there. Readers of Thomas who have never been to Froxfield will feel it right when told that more than sixty years later the frame on its post is still empty, and the White Horse still hides unannounced from the two roads that intersect the width of a large field away.

The Barnet is the eastern part of the plateau. Its name reveals that at some time the trees and shrubs were cleared by burning. A great common of 780 acres survived here until 1805, when food needs in the Napoleonic War pushed up the value of land. There was a popular route over the plateau from Petersfield to Winchester by way of Stoner Hill and Week Green, Ropley and Alresford, and when a good road was made across the Barnet it took over the Alton traffic too, and superseded the old road past the White Horse. The enclosure officials, who parcelled out the reclaimed land, planned new roads to serve the new farms. One of them, dead straight, designed on the map and not evolved by trial and error like the old roads, is the subject of 'The Lane'. The Green Lane starts at the first road junction north of the Trooper Inn.

> Some day, I think, there will be people enough
> In Froxfield to pick all the blackberries
> Out of the hedges of Green Lane, the straight
> Broad lane where now September hides herself
> In bracken and blackberry, harebell and dwarf gorse.

Green Lane, says the poem later, is a mile long and ends suddenly, and it has a glint of hollies in the hedge. The blackberries, harebells and dwarf gorse are still there. The hollies now stand up above the hedge like sentries at intervals. The lane does end suddenly. It is broad because enclosure commissioners always made their new roads to standard widths, with a grass verge on one or both sides. If we needed proof of Thomas's exact observation, and his power to make poetry out of notebook stuff, 'The Lane' is a telling exhibit.

Also identifiable is 'The Manor Farm'. There is more than one manor farm in the Thomas Country, but this is the one at Prior's Dean, where the Elizabethan house looks across at the primitive little Norman church and its aged yew, probably as old as the church and now a mere shell but leafing strongly. They all looked asleep as Edward came down the hill, and we can tell by which path he approached.

Neither Edward nor Helen took to the Cockshott Lane house. Relations with Lupton remained good, but they were accustomed to living in flat country and in old houses, and they developed an irrational dislike of this very new, hill-top one. The incident in 'Wind and Mist', already quoted, is informative, It continues

> 'Because I lived there then . . .
> Yes, with my furniture and family
> Still in it, I knowing every nook of it
> And loving none, and in fact hating it'.

The house, the poet continues, was doubtless not to blame, He felt marooned in the clouds, on a cliff edge, isolated, with mist arising from the combe. The wind, he admits, became an obsession:

> 'Pray do not let me get on to the wind.
> It is my subject, and compared with me
> Those who have always lived on firm ground
> Are quite unreal in this matter of the wind'.

Strangely he barely mentions the glorious view, of which an exposed postion is the price. The wind can blow strongly on the ridge, until tall trees thrash about like saplings, and the prevailing south-west winds may bring rain that batters against windows, and even down the hill is hard to keep out of any cracks. But the stout walker who rejoiced at the wind on his face, and at getting so wet from the rain that wading through a stream mattered little, should not have shrunk from the Ashford Hill wind. No doubt his taut-stretched nerves, which led him at one period to take drugs, and on many occasions to flee from his wife and children, were mainly to blame. In their different houses the activities of the children, and domestic chores going on round

Holly trees in Edward Thomas's Green Lane, Froxfield

him, fretted him unbearably. He always wrote with difficulty, and needed solitude and quiet.

The obsession, it seems, started at once. 'The New House' must be the Froxfield one:

> Now first, as I shut the door,
> I was alone
> In the new house; and the wind
> Began to moan
> Old at once was the house,
> And I was old;
> My ears were teased with the dread
> Of what was foretold.

This was the same disquiet, foreboding, insecurity that haunted him, with only intervals of happy relaxation, until he entered the ordered life of the Army.

Somehow, though driven to the point of exhaustion by the need to earn, Thomas made time to break in the new garden. The clay and large flints of the plateau cap made hard work:

> ''The clay first broke my heart, and then my back:
>
> And the back heals not'.
>
> (Wind and Mist)

The comment is clearly no poetic invention; it is wrung from him. This was no passing backache. Did Thomas suffer from a slipped disc? Since the complaint had not then been recognised, he could not have named it, but he suffered a lot from headaches which could have been connected with spinal pressures. Migraine and spinal pain can be unimaginably agonising, and doubly difficult to bear for someone who must earn his living by freelance brain work and dare not stop for relief.

Antipathy to the Lupton house did not give Froxfield painful associations for him. He chose the name Arthur Froxfield for the character who tells the story in his curious book 'The Happy-Go-Lucky Morgans', the nearest he ever got to writing a novel.

In 1913 Edward and Helen left the ridge and moved downhill to the centre of Steep. He was suffering a reduction in his markets due to the changing taste of readers and editors, and the Red House was too large for economy. Their dislike of the house, and the strenuous walk to and from Bedales for Mervyn and Bronwen were other factors. But Edward's habitual restlessness also drove him. As usual it was to be a new start. 'We look forward to the move as a chance of salvation', he wrote to his friend Jesse Berridge, and he was not thinking simply of cutting his expenses.

Even today the centre of the parish is hardly a village, and at that time it comprised a small group of houses within a stonethrow of the inn and a sprinkling of others along the half mile to the church. At the inn end, opposite the open fields of Bedales, the gaps were gradually filling, and Rollo Russell (the Hon. Francis Russell, a younger son of Lord John Russell, the one-time Prime Minister) had built six cottages for labourers, Yew Tree Gottages Nos. 1-6. Retired from the Foreign Office, and with the ample means enjoyed by the Bedford family, he energetically pursued his many interests. One of them was the study of cancer and malaria, another was placing small country people in homes of their own by buying or building cottages which he sold to them on very easy terms, or let to them at low rents. The Steep cottages were designed by his son John.

Helen Thomas, with writer's licence, has made her David and Jenny Townsend deal with an aristocrat who hypocritically exploits the poor through cottage rents, and the biographies, following this scent, have described the Steep cottages as jerry-built. They were of course, built down to a specification compatible with low rents. They had no bathroom or inside lavatory, but such things were not then expected in a country cottage. Geoffrey Lupton's own house did not at first have them. Conditions at Bedales too were somewhat stark; the principles of the Simple Life were in the air. Compared with the fantastic quality standards of the Red House, the cottages are poor things, but they are neither shoddy nor, for their purpose, ill-designed. They can be seen today to exemplify the friendly, unpretentious, domestic idiom of the period, so much more pleasing than that of between the wars. Finished in whitewashed pebble dash, they have a distinct resemblance to the lower-rented houses built in 1907-14 at the instigation of that determined do-gooder Henrietta Barnett for her social mix in the Hampstead Garden Suburb. That may be no coincidence; 'Rozel', the Russells' house in Steep, used when they visited their children at Bedales, was designed by Raymond Unwin, principal architect of the suburb.

Yew Tree Cottages

Yew Tree Cottages are in three pairs, two near the road, the other in the middle at the rear. No. 2 is the setting for the poem 'Old Man' in which Myfanwy

> . . . will remember, with that bitter scent,
>
> Of garden rows, and ancient damson trees
>
> Topping a hedge, a bent path to a door,
>
> A low thick bush beside the door, and me
>
> Forbidding her to pick

The bent path must strike every visitor to No. 2. A narrow path rises from the road to the rear pair of cottages and suddenly forks, bending round to reach the house door at the side. The damson trees, however, too ancient to bear fruit, were cut down some years back, and the bush of bitter scented Old Man or Southernwood, known to botanists as *Artemisia abrotanum*, has also gone. Its other name Lad's Love, mentioned by Thomas, comes from the old country belief that it helped the beard to grow.

The cottage was too small for a family of five; too small, Thomas said, to hold more than half their furniture. They were on top of each other, and his ragged nerves were liable to snap when the children were too boisterous or household bustle intruded on him. He had to get away, daily for some hours, frequently for days or weeks. Nightingales in the garden were not compensation enough. In a letter to Gordon Bottomely at the end of 1914 he wrote of an 'uncongenial neighbourhood' and declared 'all I like is the hills and my study'. Fortunately Lupton had allowed him to keep the study on Ashford Hill, and he normally spent at least his mornings there.

Thomas was not a domestic or home-loving man, though he gardened dutifully and made some furniture. His friend James Guthrie, in 'To the Memory of Edward Thomas', says 'Home was to him by way of being a temporary shelter from cold nights or inclement weather, and Thomas went home much as he might enter a wood and stand behind a stack, being all the while a traveller'. He even wore his heavy walking shoes much of the time indoors.

No. 2 adjoined the garden of the house Hill Croft, which after the war was occupied by the poet T. Sturge Moore. He and Thomas both attended a literary dinner about 1904, and Edward reviewed several of Moore's works in the *Daily Chronicle,* but there is no other record of contact. In a letter to W. H. Hudson, Thomas placed Moore with Walter de la Mare, W. H. Davies, Lascelles Abercrombie and Yeats as poets he would read in preference to Robert Bridges.

A hundred and fifty yards from Yew Tree Cottages is the cross roads of the poem 'Aspens':

> All day and night, save winter, every weather,
> Above the inn, the smithy, and the shop,
> The aspens at the cross roads talk together.

The inn, the Cricketers, has been rebuilt and now stands back behind a car park. Tom Moss's smithy, an old squatter's encroachment on the waste, was replaced in the late 1960's by a garage. The cross-roads shop too has gone, and no aspens now whisper in the breeze.

From Steep too comes 'The Mill-Water' already mentioned:

> Only the sound remains
> Of the old mill;
> Gone is the wheel;
> On the prone roof and walls the nettle reigns . . .
> Only the idle foam
> Of water falling
> Changelessly calling,
> Where once men had a work-place and a home.

No. 2 Yew Tree Cottages. Edward Thomas's third home in Hampshire.

The poet, one feels sure, is looking and listening by the tempestuous sixteen-foot fall of Steep Mill, which ceased work at the beginning of this century. Its volume of water, collected in less than a mile from the source, is due to the acute Vee of the re-entrant which, cutting deep into the edge of the plateau, drains a large area of the chalk mass. It runs fast. Aptly the Old English, before the Conquest, called the Ashford Stream the Ludburn or Loudbourne.

Steep remained the Thomases' home until October 1916, the year after Edward joined the Army. Then Helen moved to High Beech, Epping Forest, to be near Mervyn's first job. In June of that year Mrs. Lupton, Geoffrey being with the Army in France, asked Helen to remove Edward's books and papers from the study, as she wished to use it. It was not an unreasonable request. Edward was paying only a token rent, and could make little use of it even on his rare leaves. But to Helen, who knew what it meant to her husband, and how much it had done to save him from breakdown, it was a deeply-felt blow. Her simmering resentment against everyone even distantly connected with Bedales broke out, on her own showing, in a torrent of anger. She makes it clear in her book that it was not Steep she disliked. 'That heavenly corner of

Hampshire' she called it in a letter to a friend thirty years later; and it had ties of sentiment for her. It was the 'Bedales people' who were her target. Their comfortable attitudes were probably galling to someone who had for seventeen years suffered so much personal stress and money worry as Helen. She found them smug. They had, she decided, too much head but too little heart, amiable intentions but no real blood. She went without regret.

Edward paid one more visit to Steep before the family left and, as we have seen, he must have made one more climb up to the ridge to see the hills he would have liked to make. To some of his friends he spoke as if he did not expect to come back. In January 1917 he sailed for France and, before he had time to see much battle, on April 9 he was killed at Arras by a shell. He left behind 141 poems which he had written in about two years. Two he had slipped into his anthology 'This England' (1915), two more had been published in a little-known quarterly, and six had been privately printed by his friend Guthrie, all under the pen-name 'Edward Eastaway', for Edward's shyness over self-revelation not have an unbiased reception. Six months after his death a first collection appeared, under both names, and a nearly complete collection was published in 1920. One would have liked him to have seen all his work in print and to have enjoyed his recognition. It would have told him that he had found the right path.

The Author

W. M. Whiteman, M.A. Cantab.

Retired managing editor, Link House Publications Ltd. Writer on the countryside, recreation and local history. Past Chairman, Rural Committee, Hampshire Council of Community Service: Vice-President Petersfield Society: Hon. Member Petersfield Area Historical Society. Eleven years on Steep Parish Council. Served on working parties of Department of the Environment, Countryside Commission, Town and Country Planning Association. Has addressed Royal Society of Arts, Council for the Protection of Rural England, Association of Rural District Councils, Parliamentary Committees etc. Has walked Petersfield area 21 years.

BY AND ABOUT EDWARD THOMAS

An excellent introduction to the countryside writings of Edward Thomas is 'Edward Thomas on the Countryside', a selection of verse and prose made by Roland Grant (Faber and Faber 1977). An inexpensive introduction to the poems is 'Selected Poems' (Faber and Faber 1974). Readers who want all the poems, with notes, have the authoritative 'Collected Poems of Edward Thomas' edited by R. George Thomas (Clarendon Press, Oxford 1978). In 'A Language not to be Betrayed' (Carcanet 1981) Edna Longley assembles extracts from the full range of Thomas's prose. 'The South Country', which shows Thomas in 1909 responding in particular to the countryside of Hampshire and adjoining areas, is now available as a paperback (Dent 1984).

Books about Thomas, biographical and critical, are numerous, substantial and scholarly, for example 'Edward Thomas, a Critical Study' by H. Coombes (Chatto and Windus 1956, 1973); 'Edward Thomas, A Critical Biography' by William Cooke (Faber and Faber 1970); 'Poems and Last Poems', most of the poems, with commentary by Edna Longley (Macdonald and Evans 1973); 'Edward Thomas, A Poet for His Country' by Jan Marsh (Paul Elek 1978); 'The Life and Letters of Edward Thomas' by John Moore (Heinemann 1939, Alan Sutton 1983; 'Edward Thomas, A Portrait' by R. George Thomas (Clarendon Press, Oxford 1978). 'The Imagination of Edward Thomas' by Michael Kirkham (Cambridge University Press 1986) gives a perceptive analysis of Thomas's relationship to the English countryside — possessing and possessed by the land where he lived.

Helen Thomas's narrative in 'As It Was' and 'World Without End' (Faber and Faber, one volume 1972) is essential reading on Edward's domestic background, which so influenced his temperament.

I acknowledge my debt to these sources for biographical material but am unable to disentangle the crossed threads of indebtedness and therefore take full responsibility, especially as I have at some points parted from these authors over facts and interpretation, from local knowledge or for what seemed to me good reasons. The local history is based on many years of study on the ground and sources too numerous to name, including local private documents and conversations with old residents. Particular acknowledgement is due for the use of Hampshire Record Office archives and those of Steep Parish.

W.M.W.

INDEX